Contents

Founding Father. 4

Young Life 6

Electricity!. 12

Public Life 14

A New Country 18

Inventor 20

Glossary. 22

For More Information. 23

Index 24

Boldface words appear in the glossary.

Founding Father

Ben Franklin was one of our nation's Founding Fathers. He helped the United States become the country it is today. Ben was a writer, a **diplomat**, and an inventor.

5

Young Life

Ben was born January 17, 1706. He was one of 17 children! The family lived in Boston, Massachusetts. Ben didn't go to school for very long. He read a lot and taught himself to write well.

When Ben was 12 years old, he worked for his brother James. James was a printer who started a newspaper. Ben wrote **essays** for it. No one knew he wrote them!

Ben moved to Philadelphia, Pennsylvania, when he was 17. He worked as a printer. Then, Ben went to London, England. He returned to Philadelphia in 1726. In 1730, he married Deborah Read Rogers.

11

Electricity!

Ben had many interests. He opened the first library in Philadelphia and started a police force. Ben also studied electricity. He discovered many new things about it. His very unsafe **experiment** with a kite is famous.

Public Life

Ben respected the British government. He ran for public office during the 1740s and 1750s. However, by the 1760s, many **colonists** were angry with British laws. Ben wrote essays about the colonists' problems.

15

In 1776, Ben helped write the **Declaration of Independence**. He was then sent to France. Ben was very popular there. He asked the French to help the colonists fight British rule.

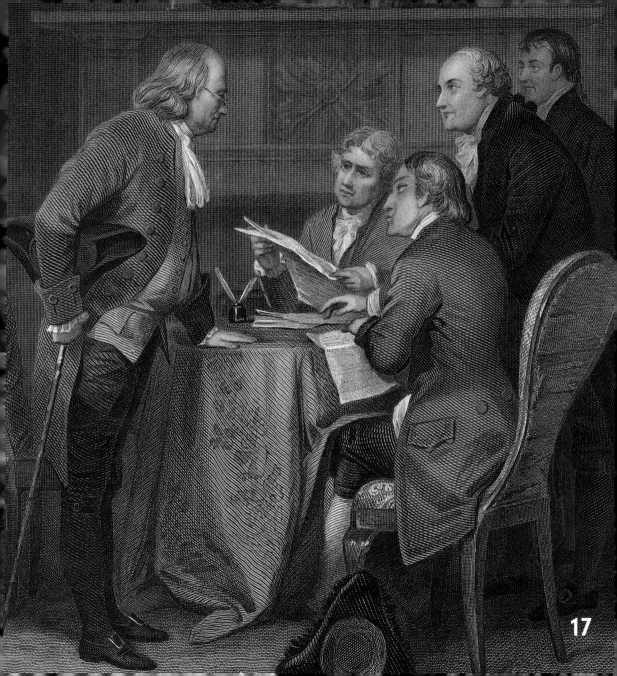

17

A New Country

In 1783, the United States won its independence! Ben helped work out a peace agreement with England. Then, he helped write the **US Constitution** in 1787. It stated the new country's laws.

19

Inventor

Ben died in 1790. However, his inventions live on. Ben invented many things, including a special kind of glasses and a stove. Today, he is remembered for these and for helping shape the United States.

Timeline

1706——Ben Franklin is born on January 17.

1730——Ben marries Deborah Read Rogers.

1776——Ben helps write the Declaration of Independence.

1787——Ben helps write the US Constitution.

1790——Ben dies.

Glossary

colonist: someone who lives in a colony, or a piece of land under the control of another country

Declaration of Independence: the piece of writing that stated the colonies' wish to form their own government without British control

diplomat: a person who is skilled at talks between nations

essay: a piece of writing

experiment: a test that tries out a new idea

US Constitution: the piece of writing stating the laws of the United States

For More Information

Books

Barretta, Gene. *Now & Ben: The Modern Inventions of Benjamin Franklin*. New York, NY: Henry Holt and Co., 2009.

Schroeder, Alan. *Ben Franklin: His Wit and Wisdom from A to Z*. New York, NY: Holiday House, 2011.

Websites

Benjamin Franklin

bensguide.gpo.gov/benfranklin/

Read more about Ben Franklin's inventions and his work for the United States.

Name That Founding Father

www.history.org/kids/games/foundingFather.cfm

Play a game to learn more about the Founding Fathers.

Index

Boston,
    Massachusetts 6
colonists 14, 16
Declaration of
    Independence
    16, 21
diplomat 4
electricity 12
England 18
Founding Fathers 4
France 16
Franklin, James 8
inventor 4, 20
library 12
London, England 10

Philadelphia,
    Pennsylvania 10,
    12
police force 12
printer 8, 10
public office 14
Rogers, Deborah
    Read 10, 21
school 6
United States 4, 18,
    20
US Constitution 18,
    21
writer 4, 8, 14